Horse Training

Acquire Proficiency In Comprehending, Instructing, And Interacting With Your Equine Companion Within A Span Of 30 Days Through Groundwork Exercises

(A Comprehensive Guide On The Progressive Care And Development Of Clydesdale Horses For Novices)

Ralph Albert

TABLE OF CONTNET

Fundamental Arabic Orders. 1

Unhealthy Horse Behaviors 14

When & How to Introduce Your Horse to Others ... 46

Don't Step on Your Toes 66

Doors and the Stall Ceiling 90

Establishing a solid rapport 121

Fundamental Arabic Orders.

Come on You have likely had your Arab for two to three weeks. You would have had the chance to train your Arab to come in from the pasture when you call him in the evening if you could have fed him every evening. Teach him to come to his name, to come to a whistle, and to come to body language when you call him in. If he has a pasture buddy already trained to come in the evening for feeding, they will be simple to teach him. On the first day, your Arab will probably follow his pasture mate, and on the second day, it's typical for your Arab to place first. You can practice each of the techniques above on different days to give each technique equal practice. Call his name on the first day. Let him get used to seeing you before calling his name. Say "Good Boy" and reward him as he enters. When you leave on the second day, whistle to your Arab, but wait until he gets to see you again. Say "Good Boy" and reward him as he enters. On the third day, go outside to the gate till he stares at you. Then, open your arms as if you were about to hug him. Stay in that stance until he comes approaching you. You might want to employ an alternative hand signal. Everything should be alright if he notices it and decides to come in. Say "Good Boy" and reward him as he enters. If everything went well during the first three days, you can probably stop rewarding him with treats and just tell him, "Good Boy," as he enters. After that, it is typical for your Arab to come inside when he notices you coming from the pasture. You won't even need to address him by name. It's your presence beside his gate that invites him in.

stance

This is the first command you will teach your Arab after his three-day acclimatization period. After you halter your Arab on the fourth day, approach him, offer him a treat, and tell him to "Stand." Then, lead him immediately out of his shelter and to the hitching post, fastening his halter. I'll say it again: if you haven't learned how to halter a horse, you should take some equestrian riding classes that cover handling, saddling, and grooming techniques. Before working with your Arab, you must be capable of performing each of those tasks. Once you've brought him to the hitching post, tie his lead rope, allowing your Arab some leeway. Your Arab may become afraid and resist if you tie your lead rope tightly. "Stand," you tell him once you've tied him. Start brushing your Arab. Give him a hard tug on his rope and remind him to "Stand" if he begins to fidget or grab for some grass. Your Arab will probably stop squirming and start to appreciate being stroked by you after a few times.

Brushing your Arab once a day can help to build a really strong bond. Aim to make it seem like your Arab is receiving a massage or spa treatment. He'll see this as a prize and typically say something to show appreciation. You'll know you made the proper choice in selecting the Arab when you see the gratitude in his eyes. Every time you work with him, give him a brush. The appreciation will permeate every phase of upcoming instruction.

Stroll

You have likely had your Arab for two to three weeks. For his feeding every evening, you have been phoning him in. You've been giving him daily brushings similar to spa treatments. He is adept at approaching you by name, whistle, and body language, using whichever signal you deem most appropriate. When you put on his halter and tie him at the hitching post, your Arab knows how to stand on command.

It is advised that when teaching your Arab to walk, you use a long lead. Even if you have access to a round pen, you should utilize a lengthy lead for the first few tries. Use your long whip as well (many have a flag attached). The purpose of the whip is to get your Arab moving, not to punish him in any way. When you lead an Arab somewhere, you should always say, "Walk," and then walk alongside them. He probably already knows this command. After attaching your long lead to your Arab's halter and telling him to "walk," you can work with him uninterrupted in the round pen or the pasture. Once you've determined your central position, have your Arab move in circles around you. When you halt in the middle, you'll probably discover that your Arab stopped without your having to give an order. This indicates that you have made new connections.

Without spoken instructions, your Arab has learned to follow your directions independently. This early stage of your training is somewhat of a milestone. Most of this may have already been taught to your Arab, but he hasn't yet learned how to perform it on your orders. Give your Arab a gentle prod on his lead rope from the center point, then say, "Walk," and click your tongue as he starts to back away. You should use your long whip to lash out at the ground approximately five feet behind him if he stops or hesitates. To ensure that no portion of him is in danger of being struck by the whip, it is crucial to whip five feet behind him.

The whip will frighten your Arab a little, and he will start to circle about you. One hand holds his long lead while the other holds the long whip. Tell him "Good Boy" each time he completes a full circuit around you once he starts walking in that direction. You must repeat "Walk" while whipping the ground five feet behind him if he pauses or slows down. On his first day, just have him make three circles, then tell him, "Good Boy," before stopping, turning to face him, and giving him the instruction via body language. Come on, give it a voice. He should approach you from the circle's center and halt before you. As soon as he approaches you, give him a few pats on the cheek and neck and tell him, "Good Boy." Give him one of his preferred candies as well. Start Your Connection Now!

As was previously said, the goal of every interaction and activity you have with your Arab is to strengthen your bond. Speak to your Arab frequently during all interactions and activities. Share with him your opinions and remarks regarding each interaction. Give him a daily neck hug that lasts for at least 30 seconds. Smell him when you bury your face in his neck. Put your chest up against his. He could be a little taken aback when you do this for the first time. He could even try to move away from you the first few times. When he takes a step back, hold on. Join him as you move ahead and hang on for thirty seconds. Before time, your Arab will start to appreciate your embrace as well. As you converse with him as needed, give him instructions. Say "Walk" as soon as you put on his halter and begin leading him out of his stall, and make sure he follows you out the door. Say "Stand" as you attach him to the hitching rail and praise him each time he follows instructions.

Appropriate Management

When handling your Arab, the most important thing is keeping you safe. I'll say it again: before following these book instructions, you must take a few lessons if you are unfamiliar with handling and riding horses. You must learn to put on a saddle, bridle, and halter. You must learn to lift each hoof and properly clean its bottom with a hoof pick. Every day that you deal with your horse, you must be able to lead him out of the stable using a halter. You must exercise caution when working with your Arab. When a dog approaches and startles your Arab, he can respond violently. He can try to kick, run, or even rear up to defend himself. You risk being kicked, stomped, or dragged if you are not alert and prepared. After being startled, an Arab may inadvertently kill a human being. You might have to move aside or let go of his lead line to keep yourself safe and prevent such a situation. It is helpful to speak to your Arab frequently in a calming, tranquil tone. This will lessen the amount of violence your Arab will react to a shock.

Your Arab will become less easily shocked by a variety of stimuli. He'll likely adjust to having a dog. He might be surprised if you have to pass a herd of llamas while following a track because he has never seen that kind of animal before. He can snort loudly and freeze every time he exhales for ten seconds. Just stroke his neck and talk to him quietly. Assure him that they won't ever hurt him. As you gently walk by, tell him he's a nice boy and give him a gentle leg squeeze. After passing the llamas three times, he probably won't react anymore. Talking to your Arab all the time will help in the beginning, as it will always be calming. If you speak to your Arab all the time to calm his worries, he will face and conquer most of them quickly.

Unhealthy Horse Behaviors
Not biting

The majority of horses might try to mouth-nibble you. This could be a loving gesture with no malicious intent. If he refrains from using his teeth, it is more akin to a kiss, lick, or taste. The horse may attempt to bite you, so proceed with caution. This could occur before you and your Arab have developed a trusting relationship and before your Arab has fully fallen in love. That is less of an issue after that. You must prevent any biting from occurring at first. Your aim should be to avoid ever being bitten or injured by your Arab in any way. Your Arab won't even TRY to hurt you after he's fallen in love with you.

Take it easy on the nibbles.

You might see your Arab and his pasture companion standing side by side and facing different directions if they grow close. Then you see them biting each other on the backs as they groom each other. You would be harmed if your Arab attempted to do it with you. It's probably safer to divert your Arab's attention from biting you at first. As your bond deepens, you might determine that a few kisses and nibbles are acceptable because of your trust. However, always go easy on the nibbles, as your Arab may unintentionally bite you. I have witnessed the aftermath of horse bites, which typically include bleeding and/or bruises. Horses can be vicious animals!

Not kicking

Your Arabian horse may kick you, causing serious head injuries, bruising, broken ribs, and other bones, or even worse. A kick may be accidental or purposeful. The deliberate kicks will usually happen in the early stages of your relationship; if your connection is developing slowly, it may take up to a year. An unintentional kick is more likely after that. Your Arab is unlikely to intentionally kick you if you don't put yourself in a situation where you could get kicked within the first year. You will know to exercise extra caution when dogs or other horses are around if you find out that your Arab kicks at them.

You will know the dreaded unintentional kick might happen if a dog or another horse is in the area. This might happen when your Arab unintentionally kicks you when he thinks he is trying to kick the dog or horse. These inadvertent kicks have the potential to be just as harmful as deliberate ones. If you know your Arab will kick at a wasp, horsefly, or bee, you should exercise the same caution if you see an annoying insect near your Arab.

Should you be aware that your Arab might attempt to kick someone, advise them to avoid approaching the Arab from the side or in front of them, and treat your Arab with the same vigilance? Be cautious around anything else your Arab might try to kick but might unintentionally kick you. You will frequently notice in the marketing that this horse does not bite or kick when you are searching to buy your new Arab. That's a good place to start. It may also state "easy keeper" in the advertisement. They don't need as much hay as other horses because they are easy keepers. "Husband safe" may also be mentioned. Husband safe can refer to either the horse's preference for both genders or the rider is a novice. All of these are crucial things to think about. To ensure the horse is a good fit, request a free care lease or a three-month free trial if you are unsure about the horse for sale. These let you give the Arab a test ride so you may decide if you want to make this horse your greatest friend before committing to it. You can start looking for another horse and return it to its original owner if it doesn't work out. It is very advised to do this.

14 Let's get started!

With the elderly man, I leaped inside the truck. He gave me a nice smile, and we conversed while he drove down the narrow, twisting road to his home. It was well known that he and his sons had excellent horses and could rope well. I wanted a roping horse again because I hadn't roped in a long time.

We turned the last corner, and I saw him. In a stall was a small black gelding with a blazing gaze.

"Has he got any papers?"

He did, but they were gone, and the old guy guessed his age at twelve, albeit judging by his teeth, it was closer to fifteen.

He was not tall.

Quite a little.

Maybe fourteen hands, but it was going too far. Standing flat-footed, I could see over him because I was short!

The small gelding had a short neck and was stocky overall, but everything about him was shorter. He had strong bones and erect legs. Nice feet, as well. He had the appearance of a small, plump monkey.

Without thinking twice, I followed my instinct and responded, "Yes.'

Why haggle when the price was right? Would you pay $1500 for a small black gelding that you could rope tie?

Yes, I could solve all his problems and profit if I had to sell him.

"What's his name?"

The old man said, "Budro."

Our first ride after arriving home was gogogo!

Minimal to nonexistent, whoa!

Budro had a lot of heat. Dancing, jiving, and chuckling across the arena. He could not walk; instead, he charged and galloped everywhere.

Now, most would advise you to ride him out. When his tongue starts to wag, he will want to go for a stroll. That's not what I think. Why would I allow him to leave sooner if he is already willing to go? He would just keep thinking the same way he always had—things go quickly once you get on! But I was aware that slowing down was essential. I attempted to show him around the arena every day for two weeks. It was a never-ending struggle of wills.

I was attempting to calm down, and he was trying to take off.

"Calm him down, breathe slowly," I would tell myself and Budro.

I was asked, "Are you ever going to do more than walk that horse?" after a few days.

"Not until he will walk," I retorted.

At last, that day arrived! After about 14 rides, he became calm and started to walk. It was incredible! That sensation of unwinding on a horse that was having trouble settling down. We then progressed to a lope and trot. Walking helped him realize that it was okay to calm down again.

The test is now to rope!

How would he respond?

How could I possibly know?

Was he detonated inside the box?

Indeed, he was.

Budro wanted to rush in and out of the box because he feared it. He would turn around and look the other way before you called for your calf.

Others would have said, "Whip him back in place," but that's not how I roll.

Instead, I decided to begin heeling steers on him. I could let him face the other way and still turn around in time to catch up and rush down the pen before the header tied the steer because he was moving so quickly. He quickly identified whether or not he was facing correctly and where we were headed.

He became more composed.

In the box, he solidified.

When I took him to the ropings, he was recognized. Following the torment they had witnessed, they claimed they could not believe he was still alive. I had heard tales of how they had witnessed him being held in a stall for days without food or drink. Budro had endured being lashed and made to run nonstop, yet he had survived. That tiny black gelding, full of heart and drive. All he wanted was a chance to get some peace.

I worked Budro on the barrels because I am a barrel racer at heart, but he was too concentrated on running to pay attention to turning. He wanted to go, so alleyway issues were not dangerous! I would try to get him to slow down and turn, but he would zoom down the alley, and I would have to rip my arm off. Feeling him give it his all was exhilarating but also unsettling because we might not make the turns. He could never lock in on the barrels despite my attempts for several months.

Although I was in love with him, I knew as a trainer that he had to find a forever home.

A man purchased him to serve as a heel horse.

A year later, I saw Budro in a local professional rodeo, getting dropped on by the man competing in the team division. The father told me his sons had even ridden Budro, and his family liked him.

He was triumphing!

I like to think that by being patient with him, I was able to turn his broken life around.

Budro was at his house. Chapter 9: Interpreting the Body Language of Horses

Your horse uses body language to communicate with you and other horses, just like you do with your Friesian horse. Your Friesian horse may be displeased or unhappy with you if he puts back his ears in response. Did you give him his grain too slowly? A few gentle taps on his neck usually cause him to twitch his ears forward again, indicating that he is not angry with you. Is it possible that he is upset since he hasn't seen you in more than a day? That type of rage is transient and shouldn't be taken too seriously.

If two horses are facing each other with their ears back, they are probably in a competition of some kind. Frequently, it's only a matter of whose horse is in the lead at the time. They might try to nip each other with their reaches. There's a chance they'll both spin around and kick at one another. Although it is not common, horses can be kicked or bit. Never give in to these kinds of actions directed at you. Should you witness your Friesian horse attempting to bite you, twist around, and confront you with his rear end, or even lunge in your direction? To let him know that this behavior is unacceptable, always move aside first. At the same moment, yell, "No." You can even state his name and repeat it a few times.

It's possible to witness your Friesian horse reaching across a fence to interact with a horse across from it. The opposing horse may take this as a challenge. The two horses will try to nip each other around the face if the other horse accepts the challenge, and he will reach over the fence as well. It is typical for one horse to nibble a strand of hair off the other's face. The area will be bald for several months. Shout "No," using both of their names to stop this kind of behavior.

When your Friesian horse and another horse kick and strike each other, you can witness a real fight between them. Scream "No" once more and refer to them by both names. An argument usually doesn't continue long, and then they part ways. It's time to look for a new pasture mate that your Friesian horse will get along with if you see the same two horses fighting daily. Your Friesian horse will probably get along with a mare in the center of the pecking order if he is battling with another gelding.

Your Friesian horse may begin to mope on the fence railing or his stall door. They bite down on the fence rail with their upper teeth when they crib. Though not quite chewed, your rail will appear worn out. There is minimal possibility of a cure for this kind of compulsive disease, according to some experts.

Some people might advise you to train with or ride your bored Friesian horse instead of keeping him in his stable. As you may have noticed, your Friesian horse can be pacing back and forth in his pasture. Comparable actions, in a sense. There is minimal possibility of a cure for this kind of compulsive disease, according to some experts. Some people might advise you to train with or ride your bored Friesian horse instead of keeping him in his stable.

Your Friesian horse may exhibit signs of excitement during feeding time. Your Friesian horse is responding to this in a very natural way. He might sprint at a full canter, stop to skid to a halt, and then start running again. He may enter his paddock before you summon him. He may be standing in his stall, staring out the window and bobbling his head in response to the thought that feeding time has finally arrived. He might be trying to say the same thing to you using the sounds he can produce.

Little by little, you will learn to read the body language of your Friesian horse. Seek out the cues in his nonverbal communication. Was it another monster that startled him? Is he reacting because there's a big horse fly bothering his behind? Did a bird fly past in front of his face and scare him? Is he expressing his ire to a fellow equine that has arrived to inquire? Maybe he's asking himself, "What do you want? Keep your distance from me. Now is the moment for me and my Leader! Leave this place now! You will probably notice the slightest tenseness in one of his muscles or a swat of his tail after a variable time. Although each Friesian horse is unique, they will all generally communicate similarly.

Posture: There are two main postures that your Friesian horse should adopt. When your Friesian horse reacts to something nearby, he probably will tense up. It could be another human, a dog, an insect, or even another horse. When nothing nearby could irritate your Friesian horse in any way, he will likewise stand with a relaxed stance. Most of the time, you and your Friesian horse connect, and they will probably learn to unwind. He'll become accustomed to the sensation of having you touch him from head to toe.

He will get more at ease if you rub and scratch his sweet spot. Finding your Friesian horse's sweet spot might be challenging at times. Usually, they are unable to reach it with their mouth or hoof. I've discovered that being on their throat or neck is typical. As you locate the place, you might observe that your Friesian horse has a distant expression in his eyes and points his head straight up, suddenly growing to approximately eight feet. Take caution not to induce a deep sleep in your Friesian horse, as he may become unbalanced and nearly topple over you. Be cautious! Your safety should always come first. When you see that your Friesian Horse's posture has become rigid, it's equally crucial to position yourself safely. He may be about to respond to whatever is upsetting him. He might retaliate by kicking or slamming you against the cubicle wall, which could be harmful. He might be poised to bolt from what he perceives to be danger, and he might run you over. Get yourself into a secure position as soon as possible before he reacts. Be cautious! Your safety should always come first first.

When your Friesian horse prances around, he probably has a lovely style of holding his tail high with the hair floating behind. There are various reasons why your Friesian horse will wag his tail in this manner. He might do it if he smells, sees, or both a quarter mile away an elk or a deer that frightens him. When a mare is around, he might hold it up to compete with another gelding in the area, hoping to get the mare's attention.

Even though neither gelding can procreate with the mare, they both desire her favor. In addition, your Friesian horse will wag his tail to brag to you, the human herder. It's conceivable that you would have to run with your

Friesian horse in the show ring so that he is trotting if you subsequently decided to learn how to exhibit him and win some awards. When trotting, your Friesian horse will frequently hold his tail up. Your Friesian horse is communicating with you in a really lovely way.

Face

When you are learning your Friesian Horse's facial expressions, you will probably chuckle a lot. Your Friesian horse will surprise you by opening his eyes wide. Your Friesian horse may display fear or fury by showing you the whites of his eyes. When your Friesian horse is afraid or angry, his nostrils may flare up wide. There are two ways your Friesian horse reacts to fear or fury. His two options are either to fight or to flee. You could be in danger with either answer. Understanding your Friesian horse's body language and facial emotions is crucial.

When you give your Friesian horse a dose of worming medication, he will likely make an extremely amusing face. They frequently lift their mouths, peel back their lips to reveal all of their front teeth, and express how much they dislike the taste. Then, that expression is amusing. We discussed the moment your Friesian horse lifts his ears back. That typically denotes frustration or rage. Your Friesian horse may be avoiding eye contact or may not be making any at all. You might give your Friesian horse a vacation from riding or round pen that day. Simply brush him, let him go to the pasture, and try again the following day. You'll learn to read the unique facial expressions on your Friesian horse.

whiny

You should either whinny back to your Friesian horse or yell, "Hello, Mister-" when he speaks to you. Most likely, your Friesian horse is attempting to say, "Hey, it's nice to see you! Feed me now, please. The other horse is rode out of the stable and towards the trail when your Friesian horse's pasture mate is removed from his paddock and your horse is left alone in the paddock. Your Friesian horse may be whinnying to his pasture companion, "Where are you going? When will you be returning? I'd rather not be by myself.

Your Friesian horse may whine at the other horses, asking, "Hello, who are you?" if you see that your stables are riding some odd horses. What city do you reside in? How I wish I could accompany you! Occasionally, you may hear a weird horse's back whinnying. Really, who can tell what your Friesian horse is trying to say? But making guesses is enjoyable.

snorting

Your Friesian horse may flare up his nostrils and give off a loud snort when you realize he was startled by something. It might take him twelve repetitions of this before he can finally unwind. It's a good idea to stroke the side of his neck and repeatedly say, "Easy, easy, easy, big fella," if that's all he responds with. This is a useful strategy to help him unwind and stop responding. He might act in this way out of anger or anxiety, but most commonly, it's out of dread of being startled.

squealing

Squealing appears more common in mares; however, geldings can occasionally squeal. The mare would usually shriek in dissatisfaction or loudly protest if a gelding was disturbing her in any way. It's wise to move away and possibly even cover your ears when you hear a mare shriek because it's a loud, piercing sound that could damage them. When a mare squeals at a gelding, it's nearly always an act of protest and rage.

Adjacent

Whining is similar to neighing, but it has a considerably quieter tone. Your Friesian horse typically makes this sound when it is secure, content, and sometimes joyful. That sound could be produced by your Friesian horse when it is being brushed, massaged, scratched, or rubbed. We mainly enjoy this sound because it conveys what your Friesian horse is trying to say. "Thank you, that feels so good, please don't stop," or something along those lines could be what he's saying. When people neighbor, it's almost often out of a sense of security rather than fear.

When & How to Introduce Your Horse to Others

When your Horse was only a few hours old, he started the socialization process. He interacts with his mother and, if any other horses are available, a few horses until then. A horse cannot simply expect his mother to teach him how to ride well. From a young age, the Horse must be exposed to people and trained to interact with them. Mainly because your Horse's development is greatly influenced by this period of his life, which is also the most impressionable when you welcome your Horse into your life; he is a little older, so don't stress about how well you trained him. All it will take is a little more time from you. You must begin treating your Horse correctly as the alpha as soon as you acquire him. Talk to him, touch him, and move his body. Assimilate him to being managed by people. Each time you remove him from his stall, give him a brush. He'll discover that you're harmless, that this is fun, and that he can trust his new human herdsman. Introduce your Horse to a variety of settings. Take him on rides outside or stroll along a path with lots of grass, plants, animals, and other people strolling, exploring, and having picnics. Take him to your neighborhood lake, the beach, a stream, a pond, etc. Here's the main idea. Play around with it, be imaginative, and show him a variety of environments, including beaches, trails, and natural surroundings. Depending on your situation, he might be exposed to a slow-moving car if you have to go along a gravel road to reach a trail.

Noise, such as traffic, airplanes, trains, and cars, could be heard by your Horse. He will grow accustomed to the various settings and noises he encounters. You might need to transport your Horse in a horse trailer if you bring him to different locations. This teaches him that curiosity is okay instead of fear of many unfamiliar and unusual things. A good horse is a worldly one.

Allow your friends to meet your Horse when you bring them around so he can become accustomed to them and learn to enjoy a variety of people. You don't want him to grow unduly dependent on you to the point that he starts to doubt other people. Your Horse will bring you both closer together, so spend a lot of time developing your relationship with it. It also teaches him how to behave with you and others in an appropriate and inappropriate way. It tells him that you are a kind, dependable owner who values him and that spending time with you is joyful and enjoyable. It's a good idea to locate and develop various mentally and physically demanding activities to keep him interested and busy. Note: You must spend some alone time with your Horse. This helps him learn that it's okay to be nervous when you're not around to form a bond. Let him graze alone in his paddock or pasture for at least an hour or two a couple of times a day. Please do not approach him, whether by himself or with other horses.

To stop undesirable habits from developing early on:

Don't be hesitant to correct your Horse.

Tell him "No" forcefully if he nips your arm.

When he fidgets when being touched at the hitching rail, tell him "No."

Early instruction on what is acceptable and unacceptable can help him become a more obedient horse and reduce the need for corrective action in the future.

He will learn that you are in charge and that he must pay attention to you if you stop any negative behavior and start a positive one in its place. He wants something from you, believe it or not. Start by telling him what actions are appropriate and what are not. Be stern but not mean.

Steer clear of shouting and physical punishment; these behaviors can permanently traumatize your Horse. You want him to respect you with pride in his heart, not to be terrified of you. To discipline your Horse and change behavior, all you have to do is say "No" with firmness and redirect them to something else to do. It's time to begin gentle horse training now. Naturally, we go into great detail about that in this book on horse training.

Additionally, show him around his stall and paddock and explain that they are secure places for him to go for solitude and weather protection. Never use the paddock as a punishment; otherwise, you risk instilling in him a deep dislike and a lifelong avoidance of it. You will quickly discover that your Horse adores his paddock and connects it to fresh water, hay, grains, vitamins, and safety.

To ensure your Horse is healthy and up to date on vaccines and worming, you must arrange for your reliable veterinarian to visit the farm. Pay attention to any advice regarding nutrition, exercise, training, and health issues.

Keep an eye on your Horse's hooves; when they grow too long, make an appointment with your reliable farrier to trim them. Pay attention to all advice, even if it says your Horse would benefit from shoes or has strong hooves. Here are some suggestions that you may decide to heed.

Choosing the Ideal Home for Your Horse

Although we have discussed much of this already, your Horse must have theHorseer housing and surroundings. We've discussed the benefits of having your Horse in a paHorse with a shelter and a pasture buddy to keep him company when he spends nearly all of his time in the pasture.

You will have far greater influence over your Horse's welfaHorse'sou own the farm. It's not perfect, but you might have to choose the greatest location if boarding your Horse. There Horse not be a lot of options available to you. There might only be two or three stables in the neighborhood. For various reasons, you might take your Horse to one Horse and then relocate him to your second choice a month later. You need to consider the needs for care, nutrition, a pasture buddy, communication with the stable owner, and shelter.

You may have to shift your "Alpha" gelding to a different pasture if he is fighting with another Alpha horse in the pasture. You must get along well with the stable owner if you are boarded. Don't be afraid to advise him to choose a different horse with which your Horse willgeHorseng. If a better pasture buddy can be found, you won't need to relocate your Horse agHorseMaking too many moves too quickly for a young horse can be traumatizing.

Where to Put Your Horse

You won't have any choice but to board your Horse if you Horse own a horse property. It is not unusual for a horse owner to purchase a second horse and then a third. Financial issues become important very early if you are boarding. You might start thinking about buying a small stable for you and your horses to live in instead of boarding if your monthly rent or house payment is $1200.00 and your monthly boarding expenses are between $1000.00 and $1500.00. If your study indicates that a 3-bedroom house and a 5-acre horse ranch would cost about $1900.00 for a mortgage, you might decide this is less expensive than boarding. Even some maintenance expenses and food would be covered by your ample funds. Please remember to account for the entire amount of time needed for maintenance. Your time for regular ranch maintenance will be much reduced if you work 40 hours a week and can only spend 20 hours with your horses. The extra time will often take up time that you could have spent with your housesitting out the stall.

The furniture in a stall or shelter is minimal. They can be painful for your Horse's feet Horse's typically made of gravel and hard-packed soil. Stall mats can offer one inch of cushioning to the shelter. Rubber stall mats typically measure four by six feet. Six mats can cover the majority of shelter flooring. The shelter should also feature a hay rack to prevent the majority of the hay from heaping up on the ground. Hay stored in a rack may get disorganized by certain horses. Those horses could need hay bags to reduce the quantity of hay on the ground. There will be less hay on the floor thanks to the net-like bag. They will only consume the hay from the ground if it is muddy, damp, covered with manure, or has poop on it. Hay needs to be thrown out once it becomes soiled. Hay can be recycled to some extent by filling puddles and muddy areas. Some horses will squander less hay if they are in hay bags. Having a grain feeder is also beneficial to prevent food waste. You should set up the grain feeder and hay rack so your horse can be Horseithout going into his stall every time. The same holds if hay bags are being used. The hay bag in the stall can be hung using a hook that clips onto a ring placed directly inside the door. It is a good idea for two horses in connected paddocks to share a clean, freshwater horse trough. If a windstorm removes some shingles or the paint begins to peel, the horse shelters can require some maintenance. Some horses enjoy playing in their stalls with a big inflatable ball that is hung on a rope. Every Horse in the Horseer needs a salt lick. That is the scope of your shelter or stall's furnishing.

A Plan for a Purpose-Driven Education Session

Your consistency in being the same person around your Horse or ridiHorsem, as well as your regular demeanor and behavior, are the only things your Horse consideHorse"routine." During your training sessions with your Horse, you shHorsenot bring any thoughts or feelings from other aspects of your life. You should always have the same mindset and conduct in a way that makes your Horse feel rhHorsec and at ease. Whatever else may be going on, your Horse will alHorsefeel safe and at ease with you because of that steady, unchanging calm. For most people, that's an extremely difficult thing to achieve.

Before you even get on your horse, make aHorsetegy for your riding session. Long-term objectives are important, but you must also plan your daily activities. Your educational sessions should always have a purpose, and you should know what you are trying to accomplish. However, plans frequently need to be adjusted without much notice. It would be useless to work on a new demanding movement, for example, if your Horse is haviHorse "off-day" or the arena is already packed when you arrive at the stables.

Even if you have just been at the school for twenty minutes, if you believe your Horse is doinHorsel and completing his exercises to your satisfaction, end the session positively. Do something unusual for the rest of the session, such as jumping and taking him for a hack. When you plug in after getting good results, you will make your Horse less enHorseastic.

The primary goal of your training will vary depending on your Horse's trainHorse'sel. You first focus mostly on his balance, looseness, and forward motion. You then work on increasing his flexibility and rhythm. Next, create and enhance a consistent contact and increase your impulsion. After that, you'll have to constantly practice your Horse's straiHorse's and collecting skills. Work on appropriate activities during a training session to support your present training objective.

Introduce variations to your Horse's diet Horse's him interested and help him progress. Circling in meaningless circles is the most boring thing a horse can do. Most horses enjoy being "entertained" and given challenges within their capabilities; keeping them interested in flat work is half the fight won. Avoid the "walk-trot-canter-finish routine" and alternate the order of tasks regularly. Many flat work lessons may be blended into a jumping session or a ride-out with a little creative thinking. Flat labor should never cause a horse to grow bored; it is the rider's responsibility to keep the Horse's mind Horse's so that boredom does not seep into his job.

The ideal duration of a one-on-one training session is not predetermined. A schooling session's content varies according to the Horse's trainHorse'sel, but the general format could be as follows:

Warm up for ten to fifteen minutes or longer if needed

The first portion of your training session is designed to loosen up your Horse, eitherHorseaking up a sluggish, unenthusiastic horse or helping a fresh horse become mentally and physically comfortable. A horse requires this time to unwind and enter a working mode to prepare his muscles, joints, tendons, and ligaments for labor. A fluid, relaxed, and tension-free horse can only advance easily in a proper outline. If your horse has beeHorseblebeforebefore his training session, begin with an energetic warm-up walk on a loose rein for ten minutes, then transition into a rising trot. This walk warm-up can be shortened if your Horse has recHorse entered from a field or paddock where he has had the opportunity to wander about freely. You may wish to lunge your Horse first iHorse believe that his eagerness prevents you from doing a warm-up in a walk at this time. When adding the rider's weight to the Horse's back,Horse'sng can be a great technique to help your Horse settle Horsea loose, calm frame.

Don't Step on Your Toes

Allowing your Andalusian horse to step on your foot increases the risk of bruises and/or fractured bones. This is another incident that might have been planned or unintentional. The deliberate stepping will only take place in the early stages of your partnership; for a slow-building relationship, this could take up to a year. An unintentional step is more likely after that. Your Andalusian Horse is unlikely to intentionally tread on your feet if you don't place yourself in a position to be trodden on during the first year of ownership. If you give him a daily cuddle, your Andalusian horse may inadvertently or purposely tread on your feet. Hugging your Andalusianhorse while protecting your feet is simple. Give his hooves some room between you and them. You should reposition your feet during the hug if your Andalusian Horse moves. Use the same caution whenever your feet are in front of or behind his hooves.

Don't touch its face with your body.

It's more accurate to say that your Andalusian Horse has an itchy face and wants to use you as a scratching post rather than that this is an indication of hostility. You could even consider this a gesture of love, but when your Andalusian Horse rubs his face against you, it could injure or even knock you down. When your Andalusian horse is about to rub his face on you, standing aside and giving him access to your hands as a scratching post is a good idea. He'll soon discover this is a productive substitute for treating his itchy spot. You'll be protected, and your Andalusian Horse will be satisfied.

Not pursuing

It is advisable to brush your Andalusian horse before putting him out in his pasture for the day once you have given him a few days to adjust to his new surroundings and put on his halter. Catching your Andalusian horse inside the paddock is far simpler than outside the pasture. You can discover that your Andalusian horse does not want to accompany you if you decide to bring him out after he has already entered the pasture.

He hasn't gotten to know you yet. As you approach him, he can flee from you. Never try to catch your Andalusian horse in the pasture by chasing him. For him, it may easily turn into a game, and it can be difficult to stop once it does. Do not even try to pursue him. If he flees from you, turn around and head to grab a bucket of grain. Once more, approach him while using the bucket as bait. When grain is presented to an Andalusian horse, he will frequently approach you to take a piece. Put a halter on him just after he enters the pasture if he still does not come. With enough time, your

Andalusian horse will always greet you as he comes from the pasture, whistling or calling out his name and offering him a gift. On the other hand, never ride your Andalusian horse.

No Retreating

When you first start riding your Andalusian horse, he could want to flee or run away from you. As indicated, this is another no-no: if your Andalusian horse escapes, do not pursue him. Your Andalusian horse will probably follow if there is another horse nearby who will come to you when he notices the other horse getting some grain or treats. Put a halter on him just after he enters the pasture if he still does not come. With time, your Andalusian horse will learn to come to you from the pasture whenever you call his name, give him a reward, or whistle. He will also never run away.

Absence of Aggression

Kicking, biting, smashing your foot, slamming you between the horse and a wall, and butting you beneath the chin with his head are all examples of aggression. After a week, if the Andalusian Horse is still aggressive, you should consider getting a replacement. To avoid selling the horse to a new owner and looking for another Andalusian horse, aggression is an excellent excuse to request a free trial period or free care lease.

Before bringing the Andalusian Horse home, you should be able to detect if he likes you. If your Andalusian horse is not content with his new surroundings, he may become aggressive. The Andalusian Horse might not get along with his pasture partner. When boarding your Andalusian horse, it's conceivable that he doesn't get along with the person who feeds him.

He likely dislikes the dogs or kids he interacts with when you're not around. You might not be able to identify the reason for his actions. After a week, if the Andalusian Horse is still aggressive, you should consider getting a replacement. It is advised that you request a complimentary care lease or trial period. It is difficult to sell a horse you dislike for any reason, which is another justification for the free time. You won't be obligated to sell the horse during the free trial term if you have time to find a replacement. Selling a horse with known issues can be discouraging for many riders.

For example, as happened to one of my horses, your Gipsy Vanner horse may develop anxiety when they walk over a tarp on the grass. I wonder whether he was afraid he would trip, fall, or slip. For whatever reason, he refused to use the tarp as a walkway. This was resolved when he saw that another horse was led over the tarp and the animal had not suffered any harm. His eyes showed surprise, and his ears sprang straight up. After that, he never again felt afraid of it since he followed the other horse over the tarp. Always repeatedly tell him, "good boy," whenever he conquers a fear. Let him understand that he won't be harmed by the things he fears. Assist him in forming constructive associations rather than destructive ones.

Your Gipsy Vanner horse may develop timidity if he has a negative encounter with another person, horse, or animal. However, if you take the time to help him overcome this fear and recondition him, it need not last forever.

It's good to show him that not everyone is the Unabomber by exposing him to horses, other animals, and nice, joyful people. For obvious reasons, you should avoid someone frequenting the stables and yelling at your Gipsy Vanner horse, for instance. Help him get over his phobia of people by exposing him to other calmer, more gentle individuals. A vital component of socializing your Gipsy Vanner Horse is helping him overcome his fear.

You might also want to show him other aspects of who you are. You can shave it off and wear a hat if you're an adult male with a beard. In addition, if you so choose (I heard it grows back thicker). Instead of pants or jeans, you can wear a dress, shorts or sunglasses.

You can even switch up your hairstyle, shampoo, and aftershave by using a different scent. He'll be aware of these modifications. He will accept that occasionally, your appearance or aroma changes if you keep talking to him and reassure him that everything is OK when you look different. He won't be as anxious about change after that.

Continue reading to learn how to look after your new best buddy.

Activities that Stimulate the Mind

Some Gipsy Vanner horses will use a big inflated ball for play or be trained to use one that is occasionally marked like a football. Your Gipsy Vanner horse might play with it if you buy one and place it in his pasture. If he doesn't seem interested, you can incorporate it into his round pen training later, and who knows? He might grow intrigued. In his stall, you can also hang a ball for playtime.

Gipsy Vanner Horses are suitable for various uses, including competitions. Certain horses are frequently employed in racing contests because of their reputation for having high long-distance speed. Although quarter horses are more frequently used in rodeo events, some riders use other horses for barrel racing. Although different breeds are usually used in hunter/jumper competitions, some riders select Thoroughbreds for these events.

Arabian horses are frequently regarded as the most beautiful animals in the event and make superb show horses. Numerous Gipsy Vanner horses will carry you several miles daily and make great trail horses. If you would like, you can ride your Gipsy Vanner horse all day. Later in this book, we'll cover more about other cognitively stimulating activities.

Activities that Stimulate the Mind

A big inflated ball that occasionally has markings similar to a football is used for play by certain horses, or they are taught how to play with one. Your Thoroughbred Horse may play with it if you buy one and place it in his paddock. If he doesn't seem interested, you can incorporate it into his round pen training later, and who knows? He might grow intrigued. In his stall, you can also hang a ball for playtime. Thoroughbred horses can be employed in contests and other equestrian events if desired. Due to their reputation for long-distance speed, thoroughbred horses are frequently utilized in racing competitions. Although Thoroughbred horses are more frequently used in rodeo activities, some riders select Thoroughbred horses specifically for barrel racing. Although other breeds are usually used in hunter/jumper competitions, some riders opt to compete with Thoroughbred horses.

In addition to being great show horses, thoroughbreds are frequently regarded as the most exquisite horses in the competition. Thoroughbred horses are willing to go long distances in a single day and make great trail horses. If you would like, your thoroughbred horse can accompany you all day. Later in this book, we'll cover more about other cognitively stimulating activities.

How to Choose the Ideal Home for Your Thoroughbred Horse

Although we have discussed much of this already, your horse must have the proper housing and surroundings. We've discussed the benefits of having your horse in a paddock with a shelter and a pasture buddy to keep him company when he spends nearly all of his time in the pasture.

You will have far greater influence over the welfare of your Thoroughbred horse if you own the horse farm. You could have to choose the greatest location if you boarded a Thoroughbred horse, but it's not ideal. There might not be a lot of options available to you. There might only be two or three stables in the neighborhood. For various reasons, you might take your thoroughbred horse to one place and then relocate him to your second choice a month later. You need to consider the needs for care, nutrition, a pasture buddy, communication with the stable owner, and shelter.

You may have to relocate your Thoroughbred horse if he is an "Alpha" gelding and his pasture buddy is also an Alpha because they have started fighting. You must get along well with the stable owner if you are boarded. It's not a bad idea to advise him to find a different horse with which your Thoroughbred can get along. You won't have to relocate your thoroughbred horse again if a better pasture buddy can be found. Too many transfers too soon for a young Thoroughbred Horse can be traumatizing.

Additionally, the contract states that the owner shall provide you prompt notice if any health issues emerge. You should also provide the stable owner with your veterinarian's phone number in an emergency. It is a pretty good deal if you only have one Andalusian Horse, and your location costs between $400 and $500. Plus, you can spend more time with your new best buddy face-to-face!

Why a pasture and stall for horses are ideal

Mostly, an Andalusian horse does well in a horse stall and pasture. Your Andalusian horse can be indoors or outside at will if it has a horse stall and pasture. Despite spending the night locked in the paddock every night, he feels more liberated. You will have total control when you take your Andalusian horse inside and let him out. The grass will grow fastest in the late spring and early summer.

As previously noted, excessive sugar in the grass might cause an Andalusian horse to founder. Your Andalusian horse may die from laminitis caused by the founder. An afflicted horse will frequently be put to death, which is an extremely traumatic event.

We only let our horses go outside for two to three hours a day during the season of rapid growth. We receive a lot of rain in the autumn, winter, and spring. The pasture is unsuitable for horses, and the rain creates pools. We only let them graze for one or two hours each day, and we don't let them out on certain days.

On most other days, if the weather permits, we might let them outside for up to ten hours daily. I attempt to let them outside whenever possible because they graze for exercise for the entire time and consume roughly one pound of grass every hour. I just need to feed the horses roughly 10 pounds of hay per night if they are out for 10 hours. Thus, all parties benefit.

Fresh pasture grass consistently yields superior results than hay, and your Andalusian horse will always favorgrazing and exercise. When grazing all day, your Andalusian horse will cover about 8 miles daily. Additionally, your hay expenses are reduced. Your Andalusian horse will consume 7300 pounds of grass or hay every year. For a single horse, 65 bales of hay would be needed if you purchase the 3-string bales for 110 pounds apiece and feed him exclusively hay—not pasture grass. Each year, you can get a whole semi-trailer load of hay for a reasonable price per bale. Alternatively, you can purchase 10–20 bales at a time individually.

We spend nearly $23.00 per bale in my area for 3-string orchard grass. For each horse, the cost of hay alone would exceed $100.00 per month at such price.

Each horse needs thirty pounds of vitamins per month. Each 50-pound bag of vitamins costs $23.00 and is sufficient to serve one horse for 50 days. At $12.00 for fifty pounds, COB (corn, oats, and barley) is significantly less expensive. A horse can go nearly a month on one bag of COB.

Horse treats come in 20-pound sacks, costing $12.00 each, and one bag will sustain a horse for almost three months. As you can see, the costs increase when your horse spends less time in the pasture. Here are some additional benefits of boarding your equine. However, you and your Andalusian horse would prefer boarding or owning a horse property with a paddock with a shelter and daily grazing time.

Give your Andalusian horse a few days to adjust to the stall.

Your Andalusian horse will have a sense of unfamiliarity upon arriving at his new home. Having a pasture buddy makes the majority of Andalusian horses happy. Your Andalusian Horse will have a partner to share the pasture with at turnout time if another horse is in the adjacent paddock. The stalls are frequently connected yet distinct. Since they can frequently hear each other breathe, snort, or whine in the attached stall, neither horse will feel lonely at night.

Building a rapport with your Andalusian horse is a good idea once he has had two to three days to acclimatize to his pasture buddy and paddock. Just put on his halter and give him a good brushing on the first day. After giving him a brief tour, put him back in his paddock. You can do the same on the second day, but this time, saddle him up, put on his harness, and take him for a short stroll. Increase your activities with him little by little each day that you work with him. Do not attempt to ride him after a week or so of warm-up exercises.

Doors and the Stall Ceiling

A cubicle should have enough space above the floor. A minimum of 10 feet is required for adequate air circulation and safety, if not more. The minimum width of cubicle doors should be four feet. Larger doors are required for a draft horse.

When it comes to stall doors, you usually have two choices. Dutch doors or sliding doors are the two options. In the event of a Dutch door, it ought to open into the aisle rather than the stall. Although they are typically more expensive, sliding doors are typically easier to use.

You must decide whether to keep your horse inside or have a top window that the horse may dangle its head over. Horses that are not confined are usually happier, but there is a chance that they may bite bystanders.

Doors can be constructed from a variety of materials, most typically wood. However, they are common in hot areas because steel or wire mesh doors improve air circulation. The mesh, though, might let some bedding leak into the aisle. A well-constructed, sturdy, and safe horse stall with a 'horse-proof' latch and no sharp or exposed edges is what you should look for in a stall.

Mattresses

The bedding alternatives are one of the last things to consider when renting an indoor space. Bedding materials come in various forms; wood shavings and straw are two examples. Which one you choose will rely on the pricing, suitability for your needs, and material availability in your area. You can get wood shavings and straw from nearby furniture producers or local timber manufacturers. Other bedding materials that could be used are sawdust, rice hulls, peanut hulls, paper pulp, and peat moss.

The flooring has a major influence on how thick the bedding is. You can get away with 3 or 4 inches of bedding on a dirt floor. The bedding for more durable flooring composed of cement or asphalt needs to be at least 8 to 10 inches deep.

Outdoor Rooms

A basic shelter consisting of three sides and a strong roof should suffice. Your horse is housed in an outdoor shelter on hot or wet days. Aim for a minimum area of 170 square feet per horse for your outside shelter.

An outdoor shelter typically costs less to construct than an indoor dwelling. They are available in many designs, ranging from open-ended bars to three-sided barns. Feeding your horse outside, in your shelter, is preferable to doing it in the barn. As a result, there will be less dung in the barn, and in an open space rather than a cramped one, your horses are less likely to fight over food.

The outdoor walking/grazing space

You have a walking or grazing space as part of your outdoor living facility. Experts advise letting your horse graze or stroll around for improved health and well-being. For outdoor grazing, 1.5 acres (6,000 square meters) should be allotted to each horse. There are no hard and fast guidelines for designing this. Remove any rocks and strange objects from this region to prevent hurting your horse.

Feed And Tack Holding

You should also consider providing space in your barn to store medications, hay, commercial feeds, and other health supplies. You need a dark, dry space to keep bugs out and your horse's feed fresh. Additionally, the feed storage chamber must be out of the horses' reach. How many horses you have to feed will determine how big this will be and how to store it. Planning for a place to keep bedding and straw is also necessary.

You will require a dedicated tack room for the secure and dust-free storage of priceless equipment used on your property. To make your tack room more habitable, include a small fridge, a storage cabinet, or even a nice chair. Depending on your needs and preferences, you may even go all out with some extra luxury features like a microwave, water heater, washer/dryer, and coffee machine.

-1: Understanding Body Language

Our bodies speak louder than words when communicating with our horses. Since horses are social animals, humans react automatically to other people's body language. However, we are less conscious of the impact of body language since people talk so much.

Even so, much of our awareness is still stored in our subconscious. We can consider how a certain person's interaction with us made us feel or didn't. On our first meeting, we could also have a "gut feeling" about someone. We are utilizing our innate sense of human body language in these circumstances.

Because the environment's resources are limited and must be

utilized by every group member, all species that live in groups need to be able to "read" each other's body language.

This implies that rivalry for resources is a constant undertone. Group members compete more fiercely for less common resources (and therefore more desired).

A "limiting factor" is a required resource yet limited availability. These kinds of constraints define a group's sustainable size. For instance, in arid regions of the horse's native habitat, access to water during the summer and enough food during the winter are two factors that limit the population.

Animals that live in groups have inevitably evolved complex body language communication to avoid wasting energy on frequent fighting or squabbling.

Consider intent and stance in terms of humans:

Shoulders back instead of drooping or slouched

Head up and concentrated as opposed to downcast or bent

Meeting, as opposed to avoiding, someone's gaze

Remaining steadfast instead of retreating

Walking with purpose as opposed to hesitating

Chest enlarged as opposed to contracted or subdued

Firm handshakes as opposed to slack or combative ones

Shake hands with someone instead of waiting for an offer.

Strike with confidence as opposed to timidity.

Ignore group member versus recognizing him; smile at passersby versus frowning at them

resolute as opposed to doubtful, Neutral with confidence as opposed to twitchy or anxious

The first few seconds of eye contact between a teacher and a class of pupils are spent by the students sizing up the teacher. Equines are similar. In addition to outward indicators, individuals (and horses) exude an energetic aura that connotes assurance or unease.

It's interesting to note that, with minor adaptations, we can use the body language that we naturally recognize and understand in humans to communicate with other animals in packs, like horses and dogs. However, it makes very little difference for creatures that live alone, such as cats and bears.

Body language establishes a social hierarchy by enabling two people to determine junior and senior in any given interaction. A social hierarchy is never set in stone, though. A fluid social structure can arise from the environment and shifting circumstances;

this is most likely true with horses living in the wild.

Higher-ranking group members typically use the body language described above on the left of the human posture descriptions. In contrast, lower-ranking members typically use the posture descriptions on the right.

The postures are the same whether we are talking about humans, dogs, or horses. A horse is voluntarily "shaking hands" when he touches our extended hand with his nose. When a dog turns over and displays his belly, he offers a hesitant handshake.

These two little horse tests may help provide some light. Keep a stick with you, neutrally grasped. If you need more space for yourself, it's there. Using these with a horse you are considering purchasing could be fascinating.

Place yourself in a spacious space or pasture that the horse can see. Maintain a hunched-over, dejected stance while standing very softly. Hold on. Keep an eye on what your horse does, but try not to fix your gaze on him.

Make your body language large and assertive, focus on the horse firmly, and walk briskly in a straight line towards his shoulder while he's in a spacious space doing his own business. What takes place?

Some people may transition from being forceful to aggressive without initially realizing it. Human aggression, like that of horses and dogs, frequently results from fear and serves as a defense mechanism rather than a means of advancing in the social hierarchy. It's crucial to keep this in mind when we're near horses.

When a horse is confined by ropes or in a small pen, what appears to be hostile or frightening behavior in horses is frequently motivated by fear. The only way for a horse to feel safe again is to back away as far as he needs to. His options become more restricted when we limit his freedom to relocate.

Like certain horses, certain individuals are inherently cautious on a "timid-bold continuum." Even when someone wants to be forceful with their horse, they can easily go from being that to being a wimp. When the horse depends on the person's obvious leadership cues and they abruptly disappear, it is a challenge for him.

Depending on the circumstances, most people move between the left and right sides of the posture descriptions on the previous page. Most of a person's position on a timid—bold continuum is determined by genetics, past surroundings, and past experiences. This also applies to horses and dogs.

The body language on the left side of the descriptions, along with emotional neutrality—another essential tool in our toolbox—should be developed when around horses.

8 The Veterinarian's Visit

From outside the stall, Doc Peterson observed the filly. His hands were kind, and his eyes compassionate, notwithstanding his advanced age.

He remarked, "She's a pretty little one." "I'll wait to see how she reacts to me."

Josie mentioned that she liked carrots.

The veterinarian remarked, "Well, I'm glad to hear she's a real red-blooded American horse."

Doc Peterson offered Little Star the carrot that Josie had given him. She nibbled on the carrot and smelled his hand. While she nibbled, he caressed her neck. She didn't mind how it was handled.

Doc questioned, "You said she was wild down there?" "She's doing really well right now."

"It's because I've been teaching her to like people for the past two days," Josie explained. Doc questioned, "So you're going to be a horse woman, are you?"

With a broad smile, Josie said, "Yup!"

As soon as the veterinarian entered the stall, Little Star befriended him and began to look through his hands for more goodies.

The examination was fairly time-consuming. After examining her teeth, Dr. Peterson estimated her age to be around five months. He explained that her weight was somewhat low, which was to be expected given her living circumstances. Her agate-colored hooves need filing by a farrier. The right rear hoof must be properly shaped due to its chipped edges, which would enhance the leg's conformation.

After looking for a microchip in her neck, Doc determined that Little Star required several vaccines. He was the consummate shot-giver.

The filly had no idea that she had received an injection.

The topic of who owned Little Star reappeared as the veterinarian was leaving.

"All right," Sam replied. You've not heard of any missing mares who have foals, then. I'll check with the other local veterinarians by giving them a call. In addition, I'll publish an ad in the Nugget Newspaper and watch the situation. If we don't hear anything in about a week, I'll assume we have a new filly.

Doc answered, "That sounds good to me." "I believe she is a stray horse lost in the canyon. The filly and the lead mare in the herd might have easily followed the river and the stream into this location if the dam had been run off.

"I don't think calling the BLM is necessary. In any case, they don't want to deal with wild horses. Please update me. I hope you get to keep this cute little girl.

As the vet pulled off, Josie questioned, "Who's the BLM?"

They are a federal agency in charge of overseeing open-range land. There are hundreds of acres of open range area to our east and north. They're the folks you've heard of as wild horse dealers," Sam remarked.

Doc Peterson had left the barn, and everyone had moved out. In her stall, Little Star was chowing down on the treats the veterinarian had recommended. The filly soon began pounding on the empty grain pail.

"I believe your child is calling," grinned Aunt Sue.

Slipping into the stall, Josie rushed back into the barn. Little Star began massaging Josie's chest with her neck. Josie laughed.

Sam and Aunt Sue approached the stall window and observed the foal and girl fussing over each other.

d. The pivotal moments

To spin a barrel correctly, your horse needs balance and to use his head to maintain that equilibrium. For this reason, we must allow our horse to maintain his balance and head when we ask him to do a turn.

The rider must wait until the horse has completed his rate before attempting to turn him, as your horse needs both hind feet to rate a barrel correctly and maintain his balance.

Your horse can only rate with one hind foot to maintain its balance if you ask him to turn too quickly, and he needs to give you his head before he has completed the rating. This typically results in the horse hitting a barrel, dropping his shoulder, losing time, and making a clumsy barrel turn. It also typically causes the horse to roll back, which costs you your wallet.

You should lightly press the inside rein while telling your horse to begin his turn so that he can follow his nose around the barrel. You shouldn't have to jerk his head away to persuade him to turn. As a result, he will just get unbalanced and won't be able to turn the barrel appropriately.

The turn point is one stride following the rate point—and never before has the horse completed a rating. The lips of certain horses feel softer to the touch than those of others. Because of this, the turn point remains constant, even though the amount of pressure used on the inside rein to instruct the horse to start the turn may vary. The turn should never begin before the turning point. Your horse won't be able to raise his rib cage and make his turn in balance if you don't allow him enough time to rate correctly.

An essential component of your turn is also your body position. You must remain seated during your turn and refrain from bending forward until the round ends. Additionally, you must maintain your position in the middle of the horse; do not sway or shift your weight to one or the other stirrup. A barrel turn requires your horse to flex his ribs. He must try to accommodate your movements if you are moving about up there, and he can't bend correctly to finish his turn.

The rotation is finished, and you have a clear line of sight to the next barrel at the push/fire point, which occurs only after.

One stride beyond the rate point is the turning point, and the turn doesn't end until you get to the push/fire point.

It is crucial to remember that before you ask your horse to push or fire out of the turn, you must first release any internal rein pressure from the turn. Your horse won't be able to stretch out his neck and gain the balance necessary to push or shoot out of the barrel correctly with both hind feet if you don't release the inside rein pressure and give him his head back. You lose important time off the barrel when your horse cannot push or fire out of the turn with both hind feet. Conversely, grass hay has a higherfiber content but a lower concentration of other nutrients. As a result, horses that spend most of their days indoors may benefit from consuming more grass-based hay to meet their nutritional needs. The fiber keeps Their digestive tracts motile, which lessens colic and promotes overall health.

Hay grows in what are known as "cuttings" cycles. The early spring hay, typically coarse, is produced by the first cutting. The cuttings become denser and finer as the growing season goes on. You might discover that you require feeding more of the first cut—stemmy and stalky—than the second cut, which is smooth and nutrient-rich. While older horses with fewer teeth might find it difficult to chew through first-cut hay, they will gladly go through second or third-cut hay from the same field.

Hay is generally easy to get. However, hay blight can occasionally be caused by natural conditions like drought or flooding. It's also possible that your horse has trouble chewing hay because of oral health issues, potential choking hazards, or other issues. Horses can have food lodged in their esophagus, much like people can. Unlike humans, horses cannot simply be helped by us by doing the Heimlich maneuver on them. Not only do they have to force a blockage through many feet of the esophagus, but the physics of that approach presents challenges.

These are a handful of the explanations for why owners might experiment with various roughage. Two examples of commercially available roughage for horses are beetroot pulp and lucerne cubes. For horses with various medical ailments, such as respiratory disorders, tooth loss, and metabolic disorders that prevent them from eating hay, beetroot pulp is frequently used to augment fiber intake. Lucerne cubes are utilized in comparable circumstances for horses requiring roughage supplements to have a denser nutritional value. To help horses chew and swallow the coarse material, lucerne cubes, and beetroot pulp should be properly soaked before feeding.

Grains

There seem to be an infinite number of alternatives available to you when it comes to pellet feed for your horse. It takes a fast trip to the feed mill or farm supply store. Selecting the best one could seem like a difficult undertaking.

Until you and your veterinarian determine the need to modify the current diet, my advice is to find out what the horse is eating and stick with it. When a horse moves in with you and leaves his present home, many things in his life will change. The hay and pasture, for instance, will differ. I recommend waiting to switch grains until there is an extremely good reason to do so, as every trial needs a control group.

Regarding pellet horse feed, the three primary factors are protein, fat, and fiber. Whether horses need more fat or protein is up for debate, but the answer is that it truly depends on the horse and its intended use. A horse walking slowly over the field during the day will require significantly less protein and fiber because he will already consume it from the grass. Much more protein and fibre will be required by a strict Thoroughbred who gets easily distracted, loses his marbles, and insists on going inside once the pests get aggressive. He'll also probably require extra fat, particularly if he works long hours.

Horse feed manufacturers have kindly labeled their formulae with the kinds of situations they hope to assist. You'll see things like "HiHigh-Performanceeed," "Mare and Foal Feed," and "Senior Feed," for instance. Read the tags always. Formulas vary between brands; for example, the amount of nourishment in a brand's "Senior" blend may range significantly from that of another brand.

A crucial point to remember is that the benefits and percentages advertised by each brand of horse feed are predicated on the serving recommendations listed on the bag. You might not see the magical benefits touted by each brand if you give your horse less than what is recommended by the serving instructions.

Establishing a solid rapport.

I feel that you have a tremendous connection when you align your energies and move in unison with a horse. You must first match the horse's energy level and then gradually ask them to match yours.

Let's imagine that your horse arrives at the school, traveling very slowly. They will probably become aloof from you and not want to interact if you jump in and ask them to run around.

Gradually increase the pace as soon as the horse becomes more motivated.

Similarly, when you attempt to focus a hyperactive horse on a certain maneuver, there will likely be a misunderstanding, and communication will break down.

Perhaps, at first, just remain on the ground and let them express themselves. Then, when you sense that they are becoming more at ease and want to engage with you, you could begin to ask them questions.

Elevate your energy in response to your horse's requests for increased energy, and decelerate your energy in response to your horse's desire for less energy.

As you sense that your horse and you are becoming more connected, begin at your horse's energy level and gradually raise them to yours. The horse will show signs of this relationship by becoming more receptive to you, staying with you longer, and being more in tune with you. Establishing this connection will take some time, but the effort is worthwhile.

Introducing the horse to contests is another crucial step to take.

I ride my little horse to the horse show with an older horse. They get stalls adjacent to each other from me. We take the horse for walks around the show field, letting him see everything. After a little lunging workout, I flat the horse when calm. I make every effort to keep things as stress-free as possible. I do this daily, depending on the horse, until it's time to head home or begin my education in the show ring (hunter or jumper). If it's ready, I might even take my horse into the ring first thing in the morning for a quick hack. Everything depends on your horse and the number of shows it must attend before you may show. Because, as you may recall, we must maintain the rhythm and our flexibility. Some horses I've taken show up to three times without them ever showing, while others only required one show to get used to the show atmosphere. The presence of a close buddy is beneficial.

14

competition in its early stages

I ride my horse to create confidence at every level. I don't make hasty decisions. To become a formidable rival, they need to have a lot of experience and establish a lot of trust. I think the German system is superior to the American one for producing television shows. To compete in the courses in Germany, one must gain the right. Numerous young horse classes are also available where the horses compete against one another. You won't be able to advance if you can't demonstrate enough success and ribbons. I adore that. Get it. That's how I handle myself and my horses. Why would I go up a level if I didn't succeed in the little classes? It is not logical. Put your trust in your horse and watch them enjoy their work. Ascend gradually.

15. EXCHANGE

We all communicate in some capacity, which we all have in common. Whether they realize it or not, everyone speaks and interacts. You can't stay silent.

In most cases, communication is understood to be an exchange between two individuals or equine-assisted learning between a person and a horse. Both verbal and non-verbal communication are employed during human interactions unless there is a problem with the learner's capacity to talk; employing both helps express the signals you are attempting to convey.

Speaking with someone else transmits a vocal message that they must interpret. Their response will vary depending on several things, but our nonverbal cues, including our body language, tone of voice, posture, and eye movements, will impact it. In many cases, nonverbal cues have a greater impact on communication than spoken words do.

Nonverbal Communication

When I refer to non-verbal communication, I mean everything outside spoken language. The following are examples of non-verbal communication: your voice tone, your speech rate, your appearance, your attire, your facial expression, your eye contact, your posture, and your movement.

Nonverbal cues are just as significant in interpersonal communication as words. Have you ever observed how you react when someone says something and their body language suggests otherwise? In those situations, most people will either feel uneasy but may not be able to pinpoint the cause of their discomfort or will trust the nonverbal cues more than the spoken words. When this occurs, there is confusion since the messages that were communicated verbally and the ones that were communicated nonverbally were different.

Many of the students struggle with communication. Some can listen and process information, but they never look the speaker in the eye or the face. The speaker may attempt to shove objects under the student's nose where they believe they could be seen, or they may say something like, "Look at me when I'm talking to you," to get the learner to look at their face.

It's simple to convey some ideas nonverbally. Emotions that are easy to interpret include fear, rage, frustration, and happiness. Other messages, such as "I feel cold," may also be simple to understand. Simple body language makes it harder to convey more complicated messages. You can't communicate the question "Can you buy bread at the shops today?" with simple body language, yet you could imitate it.

Misunderstanding Nonverbal Cues

Misunderstandings of nonverbal communication are possible. Sometimes folding one's arms indicates a protective attitude, while other times, it could just mean the person feels chilly!

Someone uncomfortable making eye contact may be listening to everything you say, even if it doesn't seem like they are. Consider how you behave yourself and, whenever possible, watch other people. Your ability to read and understand nonverbal cues will improve with further observation, which will also improve spoken communication.

Horses are keenly attentive to messages from humans and communicate within the herd through body language instead of words, which they seldom use. They can distinguish between a lion that is asleep and one that is about to devour them or between a lion that is just passing past their paddock and one that is ready to capture them because of their exceptional ability to discern predator intentions!

Consider how you interact with horses nonverbally over the next three days and how they perceive it. Nonverbal communication does not involve mime or overly dramatic body language. It has to do with the subliminal messages that your inner dialogue conveys.

He draws in a long breath. Give the drama a few calm moments to develop. "All right, Andy and I are ready to offer Serendipity to you and bring her out of retirement."

Whoa. That was one I wasn't expecting. In my mind, uncertainty is the embodiment of the ideal hunter-jumper mare. She is sixteen years old. White-pointed bay. Precisely the right size. Drilled into the eyes. a multiple-show and multiple-year A-circuit winner. She floats over, leaps, and glides across the flat. I could never find room on my walls for all the ribbons I would win from her.

She is incredible. But you don't own her. Though I don't have time to think about it, the idea suddenly occurs to me. Drew's voice is becoming more and more impatient.

"Mercy? Are you present? Long quiet is not what he was anticipating.

Yes, I suppose. Apologies. That deal is incredible. I'm a little taken aback."

Annabelle's head peeks out from behind the door. How come?

For her benefit, I say into the phone, "Serendipity." "Whoa!"

With a clap, Annabelle lets go of her tea cloth.

I turn my head away from her to concentrate on what Drew is saying. Yes, she is still enjoying her career and in good shape. We'd be pleased to have you exhibit her, subject to her health. You couldn't do jumper on her, and the over-fences hunting classes would have to be low.

"I understand."

But nevertheless...

Of course, there's a catch. I anticipated a catch. "Yeah," I respond.

Place it over me. I'm already out of luck for tonight's horseback ride. Better yet, kick me when I'm on the ground.

"Andy and I wanted to present you with a different choice."

"Like, aside from the option for serendipity?"

"Obviously." He's getting annoyed with me. If he were a horse, he would be scrapping the barn floor with his hoof.

Alright. I pay attention.

"We require assistance."

"Aid?"

We're more busy than we've ever been. This summer, we have cyclists displaying three circuits. Susan is unable to work seven days a week. I envision a scrawny little Karen, scuttling down from her studio apartment over the stables, looking for somewhere to work other than in public. She isn't good with people, loves horses but doesn't ride, and, as Drew says, can't work all the time.

This summer, we need someone to work with Matt. Someone who can exercise horses while their owners are away, display them to potential purchasers, and train them.

Matt. Light years ahead of me with horses and two years ahead in school.

Matt, the god of horses. More powerful than even a horse whisperer. Matt can smile and maintain every aspect of his position while riding any horse over any obstacle.

I am aware that I am not on Matt's level with Drew.

I put him to the test. "You know, someone who can clean out restrooms?"

"On occasion," admits Drew. "While the essentials must be completed, they are not the primary task."

This ought to be an obvious choice. "Thank you. I'll be over to ride Serendipity tomorrow," I should be saying. However, I'm not. I am on the verge of collapse. As I'm about to falter, Drew says something that gives me a huge shove.

"Spite will remain here."

"What?" I blurt out the term before Annabelle's years of manners instruction took effect. "I apologise. Would you please pardon?"

"His new owner will require assistance in handling him. She doesn't have much experience. She is paying for his education and leaving him with us.

"And you want to pay me to tutor him?" Maybe I didn't lose Sprite.

"That's correct."

"Is there any possibility that you could show him?"

Drew sighs. His voice has tolerance in it for the first time during the chat. Grace, I would like to say yes. I won't say that it's a flat-out no, either. However, it is improbable. For her to show him, they purchased him.

Whoever prepares him for those shows doesn't matter. However, I don't say it aloud. It doesn't change the reality that many people show horses trained by others just because it's not my style.

Drew concluded the chat after saying what he wanted to say over the phone. Grace, pay attention. Although it may not be precisely what you wanted, it might be better. During the week, you would get paid to ride Sprite, and you would most likely have other opportunities to show. Andy and I are hoping that you will accept our offer. You could be useful to us.

www.ingramcontent.com/pod-product-compliance
Lightning Source LLC
Chambersburg PA
CBHW052147110526
44591CB00012B/1887